OXFORD

UNIVERSITY PRESS

KU-759-827

Transport

Aaron Marks

Long Ago

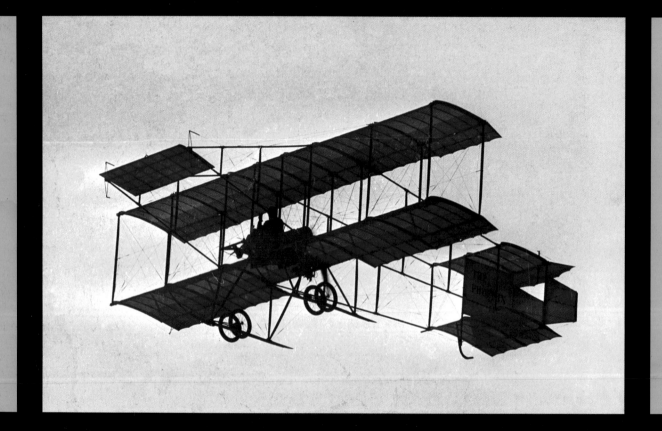

Long ago, some planes looked like this.

Some planes look like this. now.

Long Ago

Look at this boat from long ago.

Now

Now, some boats look like this.

Long Ago

Long ago, some trains looked like this.

Some trains look like this, now.

Long Ago

Long ago, some trucks looked like this.

Now, some trucks look like this.

Long ago, some cars looked like this.

Now

Now, some cars look like this.

Long Ago

Long ago, some motorbikes looked like this.

Some motorbikes look like this, now.

Long Ago

Look at this racing car from long ago.

Now

Some racing cars look like this, now.

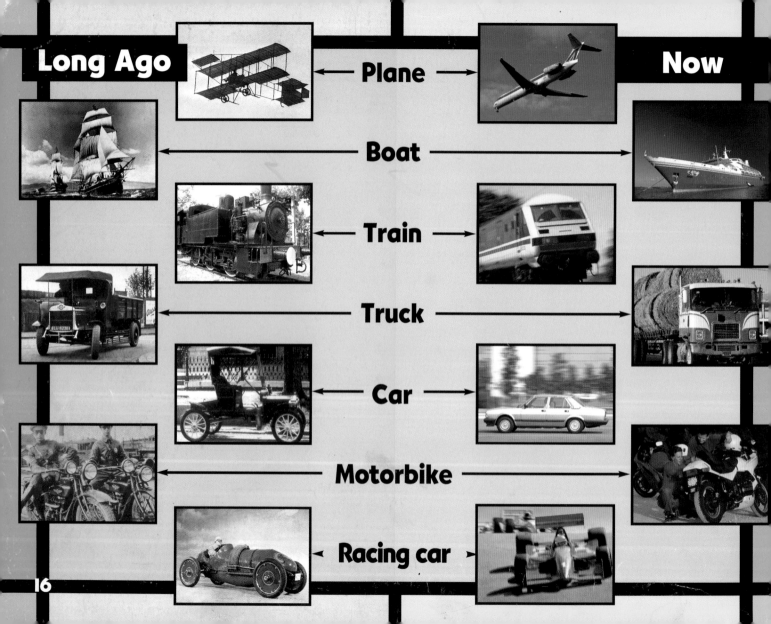

Plane

Boat

Train

Truck

Car

Motorbike

Racing car